# Stopping by Woods on a Snowy Evening

## Robert Frost

Illustrations by Red Barn Kitchen Designs, with the aid of modern generative AI technology.

2023

# Stopping by Woods on a Snowy Evening

Whose woods these are I think I know.

His house is in the village though;

He will not see me stopping here

To watch his woods fill up with snow.


My little horse must think it queer

To stop without a farmhouse near

Between the woods and frozen lake

The darkest evening of the year.


He gives his harness bells a shake

To ask if there is some mistake.

The only other sound's the sweep

Of easy wind and downy flake.


The woods are lovely, dark and deep,

But I have promises to keep,

And miles to go before I sleep,

And miles to go before I sleep.

Whose woods these are I think I know.

His house is in the village though;

He will not see me stopping here

To watch his woods fill up with snow.

My little horse must think it queer

To stop without a farmhouse near

Between the woods and frozen lake

The darkest evening of the year.

He gives his harness bells a shake

To ask if there is some mistake.

The only other sound's the sweep

Of easy wind and downy flake.

And miles to go before I sleep,

And miles to go before I sleep.

The End

61542462R00017